Kristin,
   I hope you enjoy
this "baby" book. I
love you Sweetheart.
       Aunt Lori

Christmas 1975

all color book of
Baby Animals

introduced by
Dr Maurice Burton

Octopus Books

Introduction

Apart from snakes and mad bulls that make us want to run away, animals are very interesting to look at or to handle. There are some which, because of their beautiful colours hold even greater interest for us. But of all animals it is the young ones, the baby ones, that we find most fascinating. I remember a schoolgirl who had a tame fox cub. It was quite young, little more than a baby, and the girl used to carry it with her in her arms wherever she went. Everybody she met, when she went into the village, would stop her to look at and admire the cub, to stroke it and to speak to it. It was one of the most delightful little animals you could wish to see.

There are many other baby animals and some of them you can read about in this book and see the beautiful pictures of them, which will open up a whole new world for the young enthusiast.

It is hard to say which is the more attractive of the different kinds of babies whose portraits we can see here. It may be that the baboon or the monkey with her baby will appeal to you most, perhaps because they look so human. Some of you may be more attracted to the prairie dog that kisses its mother whenever it meets her, or the pony's foal, or the bobcat's kittens. They all appeal to us in different ways. In all of them, the stories Susan Pinkus has written for each of the pictures will bring the animals to life in our imaginations and reveal to us how much there is to learn about animals that have not yet grown up.

MAURICE BURTON

Contents

Planned and directed by
Berkeley Publishers Ltd.
20 Wellington Street,
London WC2
Edited by Susan Pinkus

First published 1974 by
Octopus Books Limited
59 Grosvenor Street,
London W1

ISBN 0 7064 0298 7

Distributed in USA by
Crescent Books a division of
Crown Publishers Inc.
419 Park Avenue South
New York, NY 10016

Distributed in Australia by
Rigby Limited
30 North Terrace, Kent Town
Adelaide, South Australia 5067

Produced by Mandarin Publishers
Limited
14 Westlands Road, Quarry Bay,
Hong Kong

Nest babies

Some animals have their babies out in the open and don't attempt to make a 'home' in even the most elementary sense. Horses, cows and sheep, for example, will simply lie down in a field to give birth. They don't, apparently, feel the need to retreat to a specially prepared place. Others, meanwhile, have a home-making instinct, and will go to very great trouble finding sheltered, cosy spots in which to have their young.

Everyone associates a nest with birds—but these rarely use the nests except to hatch out their eggs and to care for the young before they learn to fly. But not only birds build nests. Many mammals—warm-blooded animals who will suckle their young like humans—also scout around quite instinctively for protected or hidden birthplaces. If your cat is expecting kittens and you haven't provided her with a cosy box or some quiet corner, don't be surprised if she turns the wardrobe into a 'nesting box'.

Other mammals have elaborate permanent homes or nests that they use all the year round. Remember Mr Badger in *The Wind in the Willows,* who had a marvellous burrow dug snugly into the wild wood? And Mr Rat, whose home was dug out of the river bank just above the water line so that the water rippled past his window? Mr Mole had a similar residence—Mole Court: rather a formal little retreat dug into the middle of a field.

Nests or 'homes' can range from very simple contrivances to the most intricate of constructions. Some birds, for example, go to very great lengths to line their nests with feathers, wool, moss or hair: others are rather idle and manage to make do with a few odd twigs which they have twisted together, or with

shallow, saucer-like depressions in the ground without any lining at all (or at the most, a few wisps of dried grass). There is one bird who in fact never bothers at all with nest-building, taking the easy way out. The cuckoo will lay in other birds' nests and leaves them to hatch out her eggs.

Extra warmth for the eggs comes, of course, mostly from the parent birds' bodies. Usually the mother bird does most of the hatching, but father may also take his turn. The incubating bird has a bald spot on the breast which is known as a brood patch. Through this feather-free area the adult's body heat is readily transmitted to the eggs.

Two of the most remarkable nests in the world are those of the weaver and tailor birds. The weaver bird makes a hanging nest of vegetable fibres, woven together in a sort of basket-work and looking rather like a long stocking. The upper part contains a lining and forms living

quarters for the young; while the narrow tube which hangs from this chamber makes it difficult for any enemy to rob the nest.

The tailor bird, as this name suggests, builds a nest by sewing leaves together and then lining the resulting structure. The beak is used as a punch to make holes and each fibre is then passed through and knotted: an amazing feat for a bird which can use only its beak and toes to perform this intricate task.

Another intriguing nest is that of the European long-tailed tit. This very small bird with a tiny beak will make a bottle-shaped nest of fibres and moss to be lined with up to two thousand feathers, collected from a very wide area round the nest.

Mammals show far less skill than birds in building a home, although a squirrel's drey in the fork of a branch is something of an engineering wonder even if it does look

merely an untidy collection of twigs and leaves. It will hang together for years despite being buffeted by gales.

Some mammals make a nesting place to sleep in, and then a separate nest or nursery for the young. A badger's 'set'—his maze of underground tunnels—opens out into several chambers. Some are used as 'bedrooms', and others as nurseries. A vixen—the female fox—is not nearly so house-proud, however. She normally sleeps in an 'earth' which is simply a bare hole in the ground. But when cubs are about to be born, she makes a special nursery, plucking hairs from her chest and tummy and lining the earth. This is a particularly convenient way of making the nest cosy, since it also exposes her nipples so the babies may suckle more easily.

But most nesting mammals are content with a hole in the ground, a hollow tree, or merely a quiet corner: and instead form the main part of the nest with their bodies. A bitch, for example, needs no more than a few sheltered square feet in which to have her babies. Once they are born and licked clean, she will lie on her side and curl herself round the pups. Her body itself becomes nest-like and helps to keep them warm. Her nipples are now well within reach: fortunately so, for the puppies are born blind and helpless, only able to grope for the teats.

Many animal babies are able to move about as soon as they are born. They arrive fully-furred or feathered, and with their eyes wide open. They can hear, their sense of balance is good and their legs are strong. But some young creatures, however large they eventually grow, come into the world blind, nearly naked, almost deaf and unable to use their limbs except very feebly. To them, the nest will be all-important both for warmth and protection. Read on to discover more about such 'nestlings'. Some of them, you will find, are the most surprising animals.

Above left
Reed Warbler The deep cut nest of the reed warbler is built by the hen, who forms it round waterside reeds or on branches, and then lines it with a padding of feathers, wool, hair and reed tops to provide softness and warmth. Eventually the nest will house about four green-toned marble-spotted eggs to be laid during June. Incubation lasts for about eleven days, and both male and female take their turns on the nest. Here, not long hatched, downless and with eyes still closed, the fledglings instinctively stretch their necks and beg for food, which for the first few days will consist of crushed insects.

Above
Mountain lion Like all members of the cat family, this appealing, furry young mountain lion — also known as the cougar or puma — was born in the quiet of a simple, hidden nesting place, sought out and prepared by his mother.

Top left
Chicks Free-ranging Easter chicks like these are at first no more than helpless balls of soft, damp down, nestling among their mother's warm feathers. Yet within an hour or so, the chicks can stand on their own, peck for food and run around quite happily.

Lower left
Eagle Owl This buff-white eagle owl chick—his down short, but soft and plentiful—has wandered from the nest to explore his surroundings. Now he is small with pale colouring, but within a few months, he will resemble the adult—among the largest of all owls. The nest itself, built among rocks above a river or within the roomy hollow of a tree, is scarcely noticeable—merely a shallow depression lined with a few dead leaves. This is where the young will hatch at intervals, but survival is not certain. Those born last are often smaller and they may be eaten by the others.

Top right
Sparrowhawks Fluffy sparrowhawk fledglings always look so endearing that it is very hard to believe they are young birds of prey. It will not be long before they lose their soft, white down and small black bills and assume their adult slate-blue colouring with crescent-shaped markings on their underparts and develop the characteristic hooked beak: but even full grown, they will hardly be larger than a pigeon, though excellent hunters.

Lower right
Blackbirds Three newly-hatched nestling blackbirds, unable to leave the nest, open wide their yellow-lined mouths, begging for food to satisfy three giant appetites. The action is a reflex one. Their eyes are now open; but during their first few days, even before they can see, the young lift their necks and gape like this whenever they sense their parents' presence or feel their weight on the nest. This action has ensured they have not gone hungry. As soon as they were hatched, the female cleared away the broken eggshells and deposited them carefully at a distance away from the rest so that enemies have no clue as to the whereabouts of the round, compact nest which is kept as clean as a whistle. The mother will remove the babies' droppings with her beak. Here the first feathers are only just appearing, but by the age of two weeks the baby birds should be well covered and will soon try out their wings. They are then fledglings. Within two months they have adult plumage and will be independent.

Above
Kittens Friendly, fluffy, cute and
eternally curious, young kittens such as
this make most appealing pets. Their
affection for one another and for their
owners is delightfully obvious. Kittens
love to be fondled and stroked and when
old enough will play with boundless
energy until they tire. They, too, are
born in a nest-like setting. Just prior to
their birth, the mother will often
instinctively leave home and hunt for a
secluded place where she can give birth.
She will only return when her litter is
some days old and when their eyes are
open. She is by no means alone in this
practice. Larger members of the cat
family will also rear their young in the
privacy of a nest or den.

Left
Bobcat This six-weeks-old bobcat is one
of two kinds of lynxes in North America,
Canada and Mexico. He is far paler than
the adult, but his fur will soon darken to
a deep red-brown and retain its black
spots. One of a litter of up to four, the
kitten will have been born in a nest well
hidden on a rocky ledge or in a thicket,
and here he stays with the mother cat
for at least six months. Like all lynxes,
his ears are slightly tufted. As he grows
these tufts get longer.

Far right
Cheetah This young cheetah kitten will
remain close to his mother and to the
rest of the litter for a long while after
birth. He has a hooded grey cape
extending over his head and shoulders
and his characteristic facial features
include the cheetah tear marks. Apart
from a single tuft, his mane of grey hair
will have vanished in ten weeks, when it
will be replaced by the adult coat. By
this time, too, the easily-tamed kitten
will have lost the ability to retract his
claws completely.

Left
Leopard Cats The leopard cat is a native of East Asia. This proud mum stands guarding her five-week old kittens. Like all members of the cat family, the mother leopard cat prepares a form of nest for her young, usually in a den or cave or under fallen rocks, where they remain until they are weaned. At this age, they look very like those of the ordinary domestic cat. Their coats are a reddish-brown with distinct dark markings, but by the time they are almost full-grown this covering will have changed to a smooth white fur splashed with black.

Below
Puma This blue-eyed, spotted puma kitten rolls playfully onto his back not far from the lair where, inside a rocky cavern, the parent mountain lion has made the simplest of nesting places without any bedding or 'home comforts'. Once he matures, the baby puma will lose all his spots and display an even-coloured coat, rather like a lioness. Originally, the puma or mountain lion was found throughout America, but today he is only found wild in national parks in North America.

Opposite
Tiger Tigers are born not only in the forests and jungles of India and the South East but farther north in China and Siberia. Their soft, loose skins are barred like the adults at birth but they are not quite so clearly marked. This cub is three weeks old. At birth he was virtually blind but now his eyes are open and he can look around him.

Below
Jaguar Looking much like a leopard except for his rosette markings, this small, young jaguar rests in the cool of the grass. Virtually nothing is known about the way the adult cares for her young in the wilds of South America and the south-western United States, except that the nest is made in the undergrowth or in a patch of flattened grass, where the female jaguar has been seen lying down to warm, nurse and clean her kittens. Most likely they are born blind, just like the litter of a domestic cat.

Opposite
Lion Newborn lion cubs are not much bigger than a domestic cat. By the time they are one year old, they are about as big as a fairly large dog, but they still have a long way to go before reaching their full size. The pattern of their coats varies greatly from one 'pride' to another—'pride' is the name given to a family group of lions. Often the cubs are patterned with spots or have softly mottled legs. Sometimes, though, there are scarcely any markings at all. All the four to six cubs in the litter are born blind and for one whole month they are constantly attended by the lioness. The male, meanwhile, will be hunting for food so that the lioness can remain with her young. The lion cubs are gentle at first. Gradually, through play, they learn how to defend themselves and also how to hunt. The males will not grow their manes until the age of three, at least.

Above
Badger Although already near to being
weaned and by now the size of an adult
rabbit, this six-week-old badger cub is
still in the nest with his mother. In
another two weeks or so he will be ready
to leave the 'set', but may well remain
there with the litter through the autumn
and winter. Until then, and before he is
ready to find his own food, the mother
will regurgitate what she has partly
digested, feeding him this mixture as well
as her milk. The typical badger nest will
be found in the cleanest of burrows, kept
spotless by the house-proud mother. She
even builds a special pit for droppings,
and lines the family living area with a
layer of grass or straw. When he is a few
weeks old the cub is covered with a very
soft fur, with his head displaying the
characteristic black and white markings.
If taken before his eyes are open, he can
easily be hand-reared and tamed.

Opposite top left
Mongooses Two small honey-coloured
mongoose kittens emerge from their
burrow. Little is known about the birth
and early infancy of these sociable
animals, but it seems very likely they may
be born at any time of the year, in a
litter of two to four. Some mongooses
will dig their own burrows in colonies of
up to fifty. Others take over those
abandoned by other animals. They have
even been known to share an
underground home, although not the
actual nest, with a meerkat or ground
squirrel.

Opposite far right
Shrews The nest of common
red-toothed shrews is a neatly arranged
heap of leaves and grass, perhaps placed
on the top of a wood pile. It may even
have a roof for added warmth and
protection, with a hole at the side of this

well-built round structure to serve as an
entrance. These young were born naked,
pink and wrinkled, but already their
bodies are developing the grey-brown
silky coat of the adult.

Opposite lower
Rabbits Most baby rabbits living in a
natural environment are born within a
burrow or 'stop', in a nest of hay or
straw lined with hairs from the mother's
body. New-born, they are sightless, deaf
and naked but nevertheless soon are
relatively independent. The male is an
absentee parent and he takes no interest
in his babies. Their mother, however, will
visit them once a day to suckle them,
concealing the entrance to the burrow as
she leaves to protect the babies from
danger. Two weeks later, their eyes and
ears are open, their fur is soft and thick,
and they can scamper about, almost ready
to leave the nest.

Opposite
Beagle Pup Young, domestic puppies are undoubtedly appealing, and yet they are not particularly attractive until some time after their birth. When they are born, their eyes and ears are tightly closed, they have a coat of very short hair and their bodies are damp and shiny until their mother licks them dry. Gradually, the pups start to move a little, and because they are hungry and have a good sense of smell, they quickly locate their mother's teats for milk. Otherwise they are helpless. For a period of days they do nothing but sleep and feed and they are dependent on the bitch not only for food but for warmth. The time differs from breed to breed, but it may be almost a fortnight before their eyes finally open and they become more active, and still some weeks more before they are as delightful to look at as the beagle pup shown here. These first few weeks are critical. Very great changes

take place in the puppy's looks and behaviour which will prepare him for leaving the nest.

Opposite lower left
Jackal Silver-backed jackal pups — born in a nest and part of a litter of eight— play near the entrance to their termite mound den. Still small, gentle and fleecy—and looking much like young fox cubs—it will be some months before they develop the distinctive slender body, more pointed muzzle and elongated legs of the full-grown jackal.

Opposite lower right
Coyote Closely resembling the jackal and fox but with an even narrower muzzle, the coyote—or North American prairie wolf—is often a feature of Western film and cowboy stories. Surviving in the plains, these young white-chinned pups huddle together for protection. They are admirably

camouflaged in brown-grey coats among the grey-brown surroundings of the den. For the moment, they are sleepy and inactive, but before long they will have developed the adult's keen sense of smell and extraordinary speed.

Below
Fox Cub Before her cubs are born, the female fox or vixen instinctively prepares a nursery burrow or 'earth', and lines it with some of her own fur. This is a springtime activity, for the young are born in March or April—blind and with a very short coat and therefore fully dependent on their mother for warmth and protection. For the male, this nursery is out-of-bounds, but he does bring food to the burrow for the vixen. During their first few weeks, fox cubs— like all baby mammals—feed on their mother's milk, suckling at her teats. Only when they are a little older will they venture from the 'earth'.

Left
Mouse Most mice are born naked and blind. The long-tailed, sure-footed albino shown here could not see for at least two weeks and was born one of a litter of five or six pink-skinned babies. Now soft, white and furry, at only six weeks he will start to breed. The female then builds a warm nest of shredded grass wherever there is shelter and some promise of food.

Below
Gerbil Even as a baby, the gerbil's sandy-coloured coat and soft white underparts, pale legs and feet, have the colours that provide camouflage in a desert environment—for the gerbil is a sand rat, a native of the drier zones of

Africa and Asia. Born pink-nosed and with eyes still closed, it is some time before the large, sleepy litter will be scampering about like the rats they really are. If the mother gerbil needs to move her nest, she picks her babies up in her mouth one by one and carries them gently to a new retreat. She does this with great skill and the babies are never damaged.

Right
Red Squirrel Although just about able to climb about on his own, this young red squirrel was born comparatively immature and a true nest baby. For at least five weeks he remained close to his mother within a nest among the branches

of a tree or inside a hollow trunk and he was completely blind until he was almost one month old. Soon, now, he will be as vocal and active as the adult, chattering away so noisily that in various places he has acquired an additional nickname of 'barking squirrel', 'chickaree' or 'boomer'.

Below
Grey Squirrel Grey squirrels babies are born in the spring, often within the drey or winter sleeping quarters of the mother. At first the babies are furless, blind and helpless. But as soon as they can see, the baby grey squirrels will venture into the sunlight and take naturally to the trees. Once they are weaned, the independent search for food must begin.

Pouched babies

Most unusual of all the animals of Australia are the marsupials, who carry their young in a pouch. They are found mainly in that country— where the kangaroo is the most famous example — but there are also some in Tasmania and New Guinea, and a few live wild in South America. One marsupial, the Virginian opossum, lives in North America.

The marsupials are mostly mammals, or furred animals. There are, however, a very few other kinds of animals that carry their babies in a pouch. One of these is the seahorse. But in their case, it is the male seahorse who has the pouch.

The first European to see an Australian marsupial — it was a wallaby — was a Dutch sea captain named Pelsart, in 1629. Captain Pelsart's wallaby was a female with young in her pouch, but the baby was so small that Pelsart was misled into thinking that it must have been born in the pouch. Furthermore, on seeing the nipples, he thought that the baby must have grown out of a nipple!

Captain James Cook, the famous explorer, was the first, in 1770, to report having seen a kangaroo. Later, when Europeans began to settle in Australia, they became curious as to the manner in which baby kangaroos were really born. Some agreed with Pelsart. Others guessed that, when the baby was born, the mother picked it up with her forepaws and placed it on one of the teats · inside the pouch. A third idea was that she picked it up with her lips in order to place it in the pouch.

In 1830, Alexander Collie, a surgeon on board a British sloop, actually saw a kangaroo give birth. He reported that the mother lay on her side and the tiny baby, less than an inch long, climbed up through her fur to reach the pouch, where it took hold of one of the teats in its mouth of its own accord.

Nobody believed Collie's story, even when, fifty-two years later, the Hon. L. Hope confirmed that he had seen the same process. In 1913, Mr. A. Goerling also saw a kangaroo birth and wrote an account of it in the *Western Mail,* a newspaper published in Perth, Western Australia. Ten years later still, Dr W. T. Hornaday, who was the Director of the New York Zoological Gardens, confirmed what Alexander Collie and the others had said. Even this did not quieten all the doubting voices, though there was by then little reason left for questioning what Collie had written nearly one hundred years before. Finally, about twenty years ago, the birth of a kangaroo was filmed. At last, there was no doubt at all.

The reason why so many people, including even leading scientists of their times, found the story impossible to believe was because of the small size of the marsupial baby itself. Not only is it minute at birth but it has only just started to develop. Its body has barely begun to form. Its legs are short and, indeed, in direct contrast to its shape when adult, the front legs are a little longer than the hind legs. Most remarkable of all, the baby is blind at birth; even its ears are not yet formed. Altogether, it seems impossible, from the look of it, for such an incomplete animal to make the perilous journey to the pouch by its own unaided efforts. But it does precisely that!

There was a time when marsupials lived on all the continents. We know this from the evidence of their fossil remains. Then Australia became separated from Asia, and in most parts of the world the marsupials were wiped out. Only in Australia, Tasmania and New Guinea as well as the Americas, did they find sanctuary.

It is usually supposed that elsewhere in the world the marsupials were killed off by the sharper witted large carnivores, like the lion and the wolf. Yet there were carnivores among the marsupials themselves, such as the wolf-like thylacine, usually called the Tasmanian wolf. Could it be that pouch-birth is a drawback to survival?

There is, however, one great

advantage. As the baby grows up the mother can carry it around easily when she goes looking for food and when she must escape from an enemy. She does not therefore need to return to find her baby and the baby does not have to face dangers alone. There are times, when the baby is well grown and almost able to look after itself, when a mother kangaroo faced with an emergency has dashed away leaving her Joey, as the baby is called, behind. The Joey lies motionless on the ground and waits for her return.

The disadvantages of pouch birth are hard to see except that it is troublesome for the mother when the Joey fully fills the pouch.

Kangaroo This baby kangaroo, several months old, is making the experiment of eating grass, instead of suckling. He is still pouch-bound and his increasing weight must slow down his mother now, too! For centuries men wondered how the tiny new-born kangaroo arrived in the pouch. Australian aborigines imagined that it grew from the nipple. But now we know otherwise. When born, the single baby, or 'Joey' is less than one inch long, no larger than a

walnut, and very under-developed. In fact, he looks nothing like a kangaroo at all and will not resemble the parent for at least six weeks. Before birth, the mother will springclean her pouch. When he emerges, he is still no more than a foetus, with eyes closed, ears hardly formed and only the senses of touch and smell enabling him to find his way up to the pouch, dragging himself through his mother's fur. Once settled, the baby takes hold of the nipple with his mouth very firmly, riding with the mother as she hops along at anything up to 25 miles per hour. Later he will be practised in jumping in and out of the pouch, always returning for protection when disturbed or threatened.

Top left
Phalanger The woolly phalanger, with its long tail and big eyes, is a sleepy animal. It is an Australian marsupial with a pouch large enough to carry the two to four young at one time. Here, a baby of the silver-grey variety—resembling an opossum—rides on his mother's back, clasping her fur with prehensile claws. Much of their time will be spent hidden in the trees or among thick vegetation.

Lower left
Seahorses Seahorses are the strangest of all pouched animals, particularly as it is

the male, not the female, who carries the young this way. The whole process of birth is extraordinary. In mating, the adult female will extend her egg-laying tube and drop the end of it into her partner's pouch. Here the eggs are laid in a way resembling a tanker refuelling a frigate. One month later, a hundred or so babies will be born, and all will be pushed out of the pouch in the course of birth. Those shown *left* in the midst of the reeds, are only one day old, and are tiny even compared with their small parents, near whom they swim. They must feed independently from the moment of birth. All seahorses—young and adult—have a snout which works like a vacuum cleaner, sucking in an assortment of microscopic animals and plants found floating in the sea.

Below
Koala Bear The cuddly koala or Australian teddy bear carries her baby pick-a-back style, often spoiling him in this way until he is almost as large as herself. Sometimes she will even care for another koala's baby in addition to her own, for koala bear families are not possessive. Sometimes, indeed, when numerous female neighbours are nursing together, the young become separated and may suckle from another mother— a rare happening in the animal kingdom. Father, meanwhile, is not at all interested and will rarely carry his young. There is only one young at a birth and it is the minutest of babies, hardly one inch long and not even as fat as your little finger. Immediately it has reached the mother's unusual pouch—which opens backwards— it begins to feed. By six months the young koala has a fully-furred coat, is aware of his surroundings and is ready to be carried on his mother's back.

Below
Wallaby A naturally shy, long-tailed wallaby has left his mother's pouch and become confident enough to explore the surrounding grassland. There are various types of wallaby throughout Australia, Tasmania and neighbouring islands, but all closely resemble their cousins the kangaroos, although somewhat smaller. The wallaby is born at the end of February and like the young kangaroo attaches itself to a teat in the mother's pouch where it will be nourished for three months. Note the immensely long hind legs. When it becomes tired or frightened, these long legs will enable it to leap back easily into its mother's pouch.

Right
Opossum This pale-faced, beady-eyed Virginian opossum is the only marsupial that is native to North America. Here he is seen beginning to learn tree-climbing. Until now he has been in his mother's pouch under crowded conditions, for the female opossum can have as many as twenty sightless, unformed babies at a time, each no larger than a wasp. Half of them will die soon after birth as the mother has insufficient teats to cater for so many—it is a matter of first come, first served. Those who do find their way to a teat then grow at an amazing rate, and the following week they are ten times their birth size. Soon the pouch is outgrown, and the babies now start riding on the mother's back, gripping her fur with their feet and long, hairless tails.

Cradled babies

Some animal babies are carried by their mothers from the moment they are born. The mothers do not make a nest and the babies are unable to walk for many days or even for several weeks after they are born. Monkeys are a good example of this. Although a baby monkey cannot walk at first, its arms and hands are strong and it can cling to the mother's front, usually gripping the hair of her body. The mother may at times cradle the baby with one arm as she is scampering through the trees.

Another kind of animal that uses its mother as a living cradle is the bat. But the mother bat can do little about helping the baby since her fore limbs are converted to wings. The baby bat, for the same reason, could do little about clinging to the mother, if it were not for one interesting change that makes this possible. Like other mammals the female bat has nipples for suckling her baby. She also has a pair of false nipples. These give no milk but the baby can take one or the other of them into its mouth and, by wrapping its wings round the mother's front, cling to her tightly. In the early part of its infancy the mother bat takes her baby when she goes hunting for flying insects. Only later, when the baby is nearly half grown, does she leave it behind when she goes out hunting and hangs it in the roost.

There are other animal mothers that carry their babies, but in their case the baby rides pick-a-back. The anteaters of South America do this. The baby clings to its mother's back with its legs and wraps its tail round hers. The baby pangolins, of Africa and Southern Asia, also use the pick-a-back method. So do the baby koalas of Australia, once they have left the pouch. The baby

pangolin rides on the base of the mother's tail, because the mother's back is covered with overlapping scales which are too smooth for the baby to grip on to.

Young monkeys, in addition to clinging to their mother's front, may, when a little older, cling to her back. This sometimes provides them with an early education in climbing through trees. In one instance a mother, with her baby riding pick-a-back, several times passed under another branch as she was clambering on all fours along a main branch. If the baby had continued to cling tight, almost certainly it would have been brushed from the mother's back and would have fallen to the ground. Instead, the little monkey clambered

over the branch and rejoined the mother on the other side.

While the baby monkey is riding pick-a-back it observes its surroundings with great curiosity. It will pick leaves or fruit and examine and even taste them. This probably helps it learn to feed itself.

Even some water birds, such as swans and grebes, can be seen swimming with their babies on their backs. But this is not for quite the same reasons as with the mammals we have been discussing. The baby birds are hatched and reared in a nest. When they ride on their mother's back, it is simply because they are being given a lift when they are tired of swimming.

Some of the lower animals also carry their babies around for a while

until they are strong enough to fend for themselves. The female scorpions can be seen at times with a dozen to a score of baby scorpions on their backs. Wolf spiders—they don't weave a web but catch their prey by running after it on the ground—also carry their babies on their backs, a dozen or so at a time.

Among the higher animals, it is mainly those living in trees that carry their young. It is among these tree-dwellers that we find the most complete examples of mothers acting as living cradles. First among these are the sloths of tropical America. Sloths hardly ever come down to the ground; when they occasionally do, they can only drag themselves along on their bellies by using the hook-like claws on their

long arms to pull themselves along. In the trees sloths spend much of their time hanging upside down by their legs and arms. It is only natural, therefore, that the baby— the female sloth has only one at a birth — should lie on the mother's chest, as if in a hammock.

Even more tree-bound is the flying lemur of south-east Asia. The flying lemur has a fold of skin on each side of the body running from the chin to the wrists and ankles and down to the tail. These lemurs glide from tree to tree, searching for fruit and flowers to eat. When launched into the air they look like square kites. They cling to the trunks of trees with their parachute flaps folded, making a perfect hammock for the baby.

Above left
Baboon An inquisitive month-old baboon, his face still pink and his body a furry black, peers out from his mother's arms and gingerly tests the ground. His dog-faced mother—the most intelligent of all the Old World Monkeys—looks on protectively. By four months, the baby baboon's face will have darkened and his coat changed to a grey or brown. Full adult colouring does not appear for a year. At first he only travels clinging tightly to the adult female's chest. Later, however, he finds that riding on her back is also a suitable and comfortable means of transport.

Above
Orang-Utan This young, ginger Sumatran ape is also carried cradle-fashion as a baby and will often travel with his mother through the forest, holding tight to her underfur.

Left
Gorilla A tiny baby gorilla weighing only five pounds at birth looks out from a nest of banana leaves in an African lowland rain forest. He is still greyish-pink, with sparse hair on his back but a thick growth on the head. Within a few days, the skin will turn to black. Very little indeed is known about the gorilla's early life, but it has been reported that the mother will sometimes reject her baby after birth—until, that is, he gives his first cry. Within nine weeks he should crawl, and by ten months will certainly walk on two legs.

Lower left
Slow Loris Here, in the tropical rain forests of Malaya, a timid young slow loris holds firmly to a branch while his mother goes off to feed. As soon as she returns, he will cling firmly to fur on her underside and be carried along in a fashion he has known right from birth. Such a cradled journey is not without important educational value. As the mother swings through the trees and squeezes her way through clusters of branches, so the baby also learns to overcome obstacles, first letting go of his mother's fur with his hands and then with his feet, then grasping her again when they have passed the barrier. The single baby loris is born well-developed, but for a considerable time he stays clinging to his mother, learning from her how best to cope with his forest environment.

Opposite
Orang-Utan This delightful pink-faced baby lies in the arms of his enormous, hairy orang-utan mother. The adult ape has an arm span reaching to more than seven feet, far larger than that of the chimp or gorilla, and a characteristic loose, furry coat. The head and back of the young, however, are only sparsely covered with hair. At birth a baby orang-utan weighs a mere three or four pounds. The adult needs her hands for swinging through the trees so this ape, too, is cradled as a baby. As a rule, though, the baby takes up a most unusual position—lying slung on the hip, but still clinging tightly to his mother's furry belly. Once he is a little older he will wander around on his own; or alternatively, follow directly behind the female while clinging to her rump.

Below
Leaf monkeys These two baby leaf
monkeys from the Holy Monkey Forest
of Bali rest in a typical cradled position,
their pink, black-framed heads lying
against the parents' arms and contrasting
with the soft-shaded fur and brown-white
beards of the adults. Within a few hours
of birth the infant clings so tightly under
the mother's body that she can run and
leap about, knowing he is still holding
fast and unlikely to fall.

Opposite top left
Yellow baboon A family of yellow
baboons, native to Central and Southern
Africa, encircle a new-born, pink-faced
infant who has yet to develop the
characteristic adult dog-like features.
They are by nature gregarious and show
great devotion within the family and
community as a whole. Often they will
travel in organised troops numbering
anything up to 300, demonstrating their
sociability in the way they groom one
another even when small. For his first
few months, the baby will cling constantly
to his mother with both hands and feet
but, when a little older, will ride about on
her back.

Opposite top right
Talapoin A full-grown talapoin lends a
protective, maternal arm to her young,
as he tries grasping the branch with his
feet. The mother's nipples are prominent,
and her small monkey offspring—much
like her in colouring and looks—will
continue to suckle for quite some while.
Most of the time, they will travel as one:
the baby clinging beneath his mother and
intertwining his tail with hers for
additional safety. Talapoins live among
the trees of the tropical swampy forests
of West Africa.

Opposite below
Siamang The siamang, from the forests
of Sumatra and the jungle of Malaya, lives
among the trees up to 6,000 feet above
sea level. Already, this young male has
the characteristic reach of the adult.
Full-grown, the siamang may stand only
one yard high, yet his armspan, too, may
be up to three feet. His black, hairy
covering now shows very clearly, yet he
was born almost naked just a few weeks
ago. Until he is independent, most of the
siamang's time is spent clinging to the
mother with his arms reaching round her
like a girdle. Mother, meanwhile, will
keep her legs slightly raised as a form of
protection and to provide body warmth.

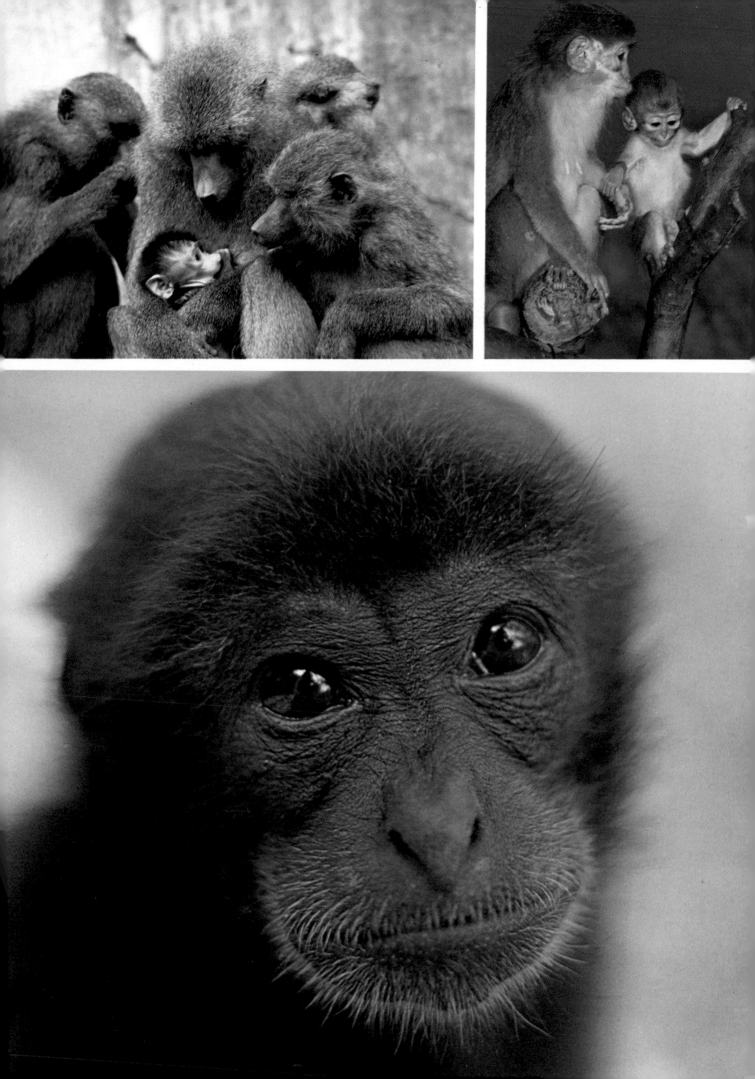

Left
Japanese ape A pale-coated mother protectively cradles her far darker offspring — a baby Japanese ape — both arms wrapped warmly round him. Monkeys and apes are Man's closest relatives and, just like human mothers, will cradle their young as they nurse them.

Below
Bushbabies A new-born, wide- and bright-eyed bushbaby is a minute little creature. Even his full-grown mother

could sit in the palm of your hand. Yet, in spite of their size, bushbabies, too, are cradled as babies. Later, they ride clinging to the mother in much the same way as the loris. Often the mother's burden is considerable. Twins and triplets are not unknown, and she may continue to carry her young this way until they are well grown. These baby mammals—they are natives of Africa, south of the Sahara, and they get their name from the child-like cry they give at night—are left in the nest in a bush or hollow tree while the adults go off to feed. Their first ride comes later. Sometimes the mother may transport her new-born babies by holding them by the nape of the neck in her mouth.

Below
Vervet monkey Just as a human mother nurses her baby, so does the adult vervet monkey cradle her young. Born in the savannah woodlands of West, Eastern and Southern Africa and one of a troop which may number from six to fifty, this cuddly baby vervet will cling to the fur on his mother's underside and entwine his tail with hers. Among mammals—and monkeys and man particularly—a very close relationship exists between mother and child. This relationship is essential for healthy development. Experimentation with orphan monkeys and artificial 'mothers' consisting of wire and covered with towelling have shown the babies will cling to this substitute 'mother' figure for both security and warmth.

Water babies

Animals that spend all their time in water are said to be aquatic. They include all the fishes, apart from the mudskippers of South East Asia, which spend nearly as much time out of the water as in it. Then there are many insects that spend their larval life wholly in the water and some, such as the diving beetles, water beetles and water boatmen, that seldom leave the water although as adults they can fly. There are other lower forms of life that never leave the water. In the sea, especially, there are all the jelly-fishes, sea anemones, corals, worms, molluscs, as well as crustaceans.

Among the higher forms of life— for example, the frogs, toads, sala-manders and newts, reptiles, birds and mammals—very few of the verte-brates are wholly aquatic. There are, for example, no more than a handful of frogs and toads that stay in the water all their lives and there is at least one frog that never goes near the water even to lay its eggs. A few salamanders spend their whole life in the water. So do the marine turtles. Crocodiles come very near to doing so but they also spend quite a lot of time on the land and, like the turtles, must leave the water to lay their eggs. All whales are wholly aquatic, so are the sea cows, of which there are two kinds, the manatee and the dugong. Most seals spend more than half their time in the water hunting their food. Some even sleep in the water.

There are many other mammals and quite a few birds that are aquatic or, at any rate, semi-aquatic, living some of the time on the land and some of the time in the water. A number of their young will be featured in this section devoted to the 'water babies'. A few, you will find, are quite literally born-swimmers, and are at home in the

water within only a few moments of birth. Others take to the water more reluctantly, and have to be taught to swim by a parent, who in some cases may resort to pushing them in. Some, like penguins and polar bears, must quickly acclima-tize to freezing Arctic and Antarctic regions. For others, like the hippos of Africa, the waters of a natural habitat are warm and inviting.

In Europe, including Britain, there is a rodent known as the water vole. It is often called the water rat, because it looks like a rat. If we take a closer look at the water vole we see it has very small eyes. Its ears are also very small and are almost hidden in its fur. The muzzle is blunt.

Anyone who has studied the water vole knows that it has a burrow in the bank of a river, stream or lake. It sleeps on land, it feeds on land or on the vegetation at the edge of the water. It breeds on land and its babies do not enter the water until they are nearly old enough to leave their mother. Indeed, a water vole uses water largely to go from one feeding ground to another or to escape from its enemies. It is, of course, a most skilful swimmer and diver.

Yet watch a water vole running along the land near the edge of the water. Every now and then, where the margin of the land is more steep than elsewhere, it will tumble into the water. It quickly scrambles out onto land again as if it can hardly bear to be in the water. We could justly say, in spite of its prowess in swimming—and especially in diving— that a water vole is only just semi-aquatic. Moreover, in some parts of the continent of Europe the rodent known in English as the water vole never goes near the water!

Much the same sort of thing applies to the water shrew. The

water shrew is an even more expert swimmer than the water vole. Its toes are fringed with hairs so that each foot forms a paddle and its tail has a line of hairs on the underside, forming a sort of keel, so that it makes an excellent steering mechanism. When living near the water the shrew gets most of its food from the water, where it hunts insect larvae, fish and other fully aquatic animals. While most aquatic or semi-aquatic animals have a waterproof fur, the water shrew must run through one of its burrows on the land to squeeze the water from its coat. If it is unable to do this it soon dies from exposure. Furthermore, it is not unusual to find shrews living many miles from the nearest water.

The otter, of all the mammals, we think of as a water animal living an aquatic life. Yet its story is like that of the water vole and the water shrew, except that the otter is even

more adapted to its aquatic life. It has webbed hind feet, a powerful tail used as a rudder, waterproof fur and a number of other features that fit it for its life in the water.

But the baby otter, too, behaves as if it were destined to be a land animal. It has to be coaxed into the water by its mother, although once in the water it is soon able to swim.

When, as in this section, we deal with what are called 'water babies', we are dealing with those land animals that have taken again to using water. They are the animal babies that will use the fresh waters or the sea as a means of livelihood.

also one of the most fascinating, with a remarkable affinity to the mother. As soon as the young are hatched, the adult female calls and the ducklings follow at once. Her call is familiar: they heard it while still in their shells, from which they could be heard cheeping back. Mallards often nest on the ground, but at times will go higher and build nests in trees of up to 50 ft. Once the eggs are hatched the mother flies down and calls from the ground. The young cannot fly but they follow her, responding to the call, and fall quite fearlessly, to land unharmed alongside the mother bird. Very soon they will be ready to take to the water.

Left
Coots A mother coot tends her brood of six downy young. They are only one month old, but already they have taken to the water and can dive and look for food. Watch for them in spring— throughout Europe, Australia, Russia, Northern China, India, Cyprus and North Africa. The adult coots do not recognize their chicks until a fortnight after they are hatched. Most are born in nests at the edge of ponds and lakes and are cared for by the male who tends to feed any chick at all who looks like his own. He ignores only those too old or too small to be part of his brood. Two weeks later, however, the adults are well able to distinguish their young, even though to human eyes they appear identical. Except for the central forehead, which is bare, the chick is covered in the very softest black down,

with a furry grey underpart and bright orange-red markings on the sides of the neck and chin. Compare this coat with the adult's more sombre colouring.

Below left
Fairy Tern A tiny fairy tern chick, hatched in the Seychelles, awaits the return of his mother to the nest. At first he is far too young to catch his own fish, but once he has learnt to fly, he will dive for food whenever he spots a movement in the water. This, too, is a water baby. Unlike other terns, which tend to nest on the ground, the fairy tern will nest in a bush or small tree, usually in central regions of the Pacific. A single egg is laid and then left to rest on a branch scarcely wider than the egg itself. Here the adult sits during incubation in a miraculous balancing act. Once hatched, the

youngster stays hidden in the foliage for several days, clinging to the branch with his strong claws until eventually it either jumps or falls to the ground by accident. It is then ready to take to the water, and is soon thoroughly at home.

Below
Cygnets Swans and their cygnets contrast markedly in appearance, but both are equally attractive. The nestlings— greyish balls of fluff with paler underparts and a shiny black bill—have yet to develop the sophisticated adult plumage. Yet within only five months they should be fully fledged. Between four and twelve eggs are laid in a cone-shaped nest of stems, roots and water reeds, and here the brood will be cared for and conscientiously protected by both parents.

Left
Penguins The penguin—a flightless bird, like the emu—does in fact have wings, but they are used only as paddles for swimming, a skill which the young soon develop. In their natural habitat, some penguins nest by the sea. Others—the King and Emperor Penguins among them—lay a single egg which the parent holds on its feet protected by a fold of skin in front of the body. Here the tiny chick will remain until it is old enough to withstand Antarctic weather. The Gentoo penguin—shown left with two of its young—nests high in the cliffs in the region of the Falkland Islands and elsewhere in the sub-Antarctic. From eggs which are hatched in the first week of December, the chicks emerge shyly, hardly four inches high and covered in thick, light-grey feathers except for a soft, white front. They don't develop the smart, smooth adult coat, nor the characteristic white eye patch of the full-grown Gentoo for some weeks.

Below
Gannets Most birds have a 'brood patch' a bare spot where feathers have dropped out at the beginning of the breeding season, enabling the eggs to be warmed by the mother's body. The gannet, however, is different. The adults do not have this patch, and so their single eggs must be incubated in another way—between the webbed feet. The young are born naked, in nests on flat-topped off-shore islands. A luxurious coat of fluffy, milk-white down soon develops and forms a direct contrast with the bright black beak, which is later replaced by the adult yellow bill. Gannets are poor parents. At only two months, the young are abandoned. However, they soon learn to fend for themselves.

Opposite
Kittiwakes The kittiwake is a species of small gull. It breeds, like many birds, in colony formation, but in a most unusual habitat—always on the high, very narrow ledges of cliffs bordering the sea. Nests of grass and seaweed, packed together with mud, are built solidly in an instinctive attempt to prevent the eggs from falling during three weeks' incubation. Once the chicks emerge, sharp claws and strong toes help them hold fast to this precarious nesting place, but they cannot exercise their wings for fear of losing balance.

Above

Hippo The hippo is a natural swimmer right from the start. A zoologist who witnessed the birth of a hippo in the wild, said the young creature immediately ran off as he approached, making for the water's edge and jumping straight in without the slightest hesitation. The hippo may even be born in shallow water, and within five minutes the enormous yet playful baby is both walking and swimming. He will also suckle under water, coming to the surface every now and then to take in a deep breath of air. Yet, just like the female otter, the mother hippo may sometimes have to give her baby a helping shove. A film made in Moscow zoo showed a newly-born hippo climbing on to his mother's muzzle, from where he was thrown into the water. At birth, young hippos may seem large enough, but they are only about one quarter of the mother's 14 ft. length, and weigh only 60 lbs. compared with a possible full adult four tons. Out of the water, they will be cared for at times in a crèche or nursery system. While the mothers go to pasture, the young are cared for by a group of female 'aunts' who protect them from the possible dangerous attacks of older males.

Right

Polar bear Cubs like the fluffy youngster shown here make fine swimmers instinctively. A zoo superintendent in Prague proved this when he hand-reared a cub in his apartment. On the 138th day, he took it to a bear run and immediately the baby was able both to swim and dive. Normally, during the first four or five months, the cub will be cared for constantly by his mother. This is essential. For all of 70 days, the cub is unable to walk by himself, let alone swim: and hearing and sight take time to develop. The young polar bear is born completely furred with short, warm hair to protect him from the cold; but he is really no more than a tiny, unevenly-shaped ball—only as long as a 12-inch ruler and weighing as little as 1½ lbs, nowhere approaching the full adult half-ton. Only rarely in the animal kingdom do we find such a contrast in size between parent and offspring. The lair is prepared before birth, either in the snow or among rocks, and here the mother stays for as long as she is suckling. Her body fat stores are sufficient to enable her to survive without hunting during this time. For the first seven weeks the cubs must be fed every other hour by day and three-hourly by night.

Left
Water vole A very young water vole
ventures into the open and daringly tries
the water. Baby water voles—like otters—
are scared of their natural adult habitat.
A naturalist who has kept them as pets
reports that when placed in water a new-
born vole will scream out loud, protesting
until removed. By the third week,
however, the water vole is independent,
feeding by itself and swimming strongly.
The vole, like the hippo, is encouraged to
swim beside his mother's shoulder or at
least to keep close behind her until he is
proficient.

Below
Seal This appealing Southern fur seal
pup is not yet four months old. The
short curled hairs of his velvety black coat
glisten brightly but soon he will moult and
grow a brand new olive-grey covering
with a thick brown underfur. A year
later he will exchange it yet again for a
silver-grey covering. Born mid-winter,
usually in December, the baby Southern
seal measures 2 ft. 6 ins. from nose to tail
and weighs about 14 lbs. But by the time
he is grown, the male will be three times
this length and 32 times the weight, and
the female will be twice the length and
about 15 times as heavy. Within one
hour of birth the seal begins to suckle,
and stays close by the mother for a week
or so. Soon he will go to sea—only for a
day or two at first, but gradually
increasing the time he spends away until
at two months old he can survive on his
own for all of two weeks.

Right
Otter Mother and baby otter bask in the
sun together, for the moment away from
the water. Now it is warm, but later the
heat of the mother's body will provide
an all-important protection in more wintry
weather. Little is known about the otter's
actual birth, but for two months the cub
remains in the nest to be suckled by the
female, whose job it is to rear it. The
males take no interest at all in the cubs'
rather slow development. Although they
become agile swimmers, at this early age
the cubs will do anything they can to
avoid the water. They prefer to give way
to an urge to climb. This is just as well,
as they still have insufficient waterproof
under-fur to provide any buoyancy.
A month or so later, however, the mother
instinctively takes on the task of
instructor in both swimming and
hunting. Usually a little blackmail
becomes necessary, and the mother may
well withhold food until the cubs enter
the water. Sometimes she even goes so
far as to push them in.

Walk-about babies

Some animals are alert and able to walk about within a few minutes of their birth. We have called these the 'walk-about' babies.

This very rapid development of their powers of movement is, of course, a protective device. It enables them to keep up with their mothers if sudden dangers threaten. Usually, this very rapid development is associated with animals who depend on fleet-footedness to escape from an enemy. But birds as well as animals differ considerably in their rate of development. Some birds can run about and feed themselves soon after they are hatched. Others are helpless for several weeks.

Imagine you are out on the grasslands of East Africa. The sun is blazing down. Insects buzz and all the sounds of this wild and untouched part of the earth are thrumming in your ears. It is so hot that the grasslands seem to quiver. A baby waterbuck has just been born. For a few moments it lies helpless there on the ground—wrapped in its birth membrane or skin, just as it was inside the mother's body. These birth membranes are as fine as tissue paper although very much tougher. Now the mother is busy licking her baby. With her tongue she tears the membranes and as she licks she swallows them, until the baby is free. The mother then continues licking, to dry the baby's hairy body. If she did not do this the baby would suffer from the cold. When a liquid evaporates from a surface, that surface cools. We feel this when we get out of the water after bathing. Although the day may be warm, the heat of our body makes the water on our skin start to evaporate. Unless we quickly dry ourselves with a towel we begin to shiver.

For many months, the baby waterbuck has been inside the mother's body living in a constant temperature. Now it is without that warmth, and if it is born in the evening or during the night, when the air temperature has dropped, it is likely to suffer from the cold.

The waterbuck is an antelope, a relative of cows and sheep that live in the cooler parts of the world. Their babies especially need protection from the sudden change of temperature. Not only does the mother lick them dry, but also the baby has inside it an emergency supply of heat known as brown fat. This lies under the skin around the shoulders and the neck.

Ordinary white fat represents stored food that can be converted into energy and heat. This conversion works fairly slowly. Brown fat, on the other hand, can be converted into heat very rapidly, and this happens when the body containing it begins to grow cold. This process is rather like switching on an electric blanket. The way brown fat works has only been realized within the last few years, so it is not yet known how many animals have it. Only mammals have it, and usually only baby mammals, though the adults of a few species seem to have it also.

Possibly the brown fat gives energy for other uses. The baby antelope, soon after it has been licked clean, starts trying to get onto its feet. Its first attempts to do so are feeble and after trying it sinks back into a crouching position, rests awhile, then tries again. After a time it manages to rise up onto all fours. It wobbles a little, perhaps collapsing once or twice, but finally it manages to stay up, still a little uncertain of itself but rapidly getting stronger on its legs.

Within an hour or so the baby waterbuck will be able to walk and within twenty-four hours it can run beside its mother. Once it is able to walk it starts to nose around between the mother's legs, for her teats. It takes its first feed.

Some baby animals do not attempt to walk until they are weeks old. Young antelopes, cattle and sheep, as well as the young of other hoofed animals cannot afford to wait. Their mothers have to be on the move to find fresh pasture and their babies must move with them. And then, as we have said, there is always the danger that the herds in which they live may have to run to escape an enemy.

Above
Giraffe Silhouetted against a soft blue sky in the savannah of Africa, the long-necked mother giraffe and her offspring stand proud and erect. For a calf, the baby is enormous: all of six feet

high at birth, hornless as yet but with a fine, furry mane. One young giraffe, born in the National Zoo of Washington DC, stood upright only five minutes after birth. This was a rarity, but most new-born giraffes rise from the ground within an hour. The birth process itself is remarkable. The mother will literally 'drop' her calf from a standing position, which means a fall of about seven feet for the fortunately hardy baby. In many respects, the baby giraffe is already self-sufficient; but these are early days, and for some time he is suckled and cared for in a crêche system, enjoying the company and protection of other calves and adults.

Right
Mouflon This new-born mouflon or wild sheep, found mainly in Sardinia, is only a few hours old, yet − a truly precocious baby − he is already on his feet, gingerly testing the ground. Although frequently interbred with domesticated sheep, the pure-strain mouflon is often pale honey-coloured as here.

Above
Fallow fawn The fallow fawn is also wide-awake. His pinkish nose and ears and his shining eyes are alert at only one day old. Although he can walk as soon as he is born his mother often leaves him in dense vegetation while she hunts for food. Among brown leaves and branches, his fine dappled coat is virtually invisible— a splendid example of nature's way of providing inbuilt protection.

Right
Reindeer The young reindeer calf stands close by his mother—very different in appearance and the only female deer to grow antlers. It has taken this baby only an hour to learn to stand. Soon he will be firm enough on his feet to travel with his mother. Such early maturity proves useful. Long legs and a short body will assist him in escaping from his natural enemy, the wolf.

Opposite
Deer This week-old roe kid, born in the month of May, stands only as high as the bluebells surrounding him. His coat is a warm red, with rows of cream-white spots on the flanks, but by winter he will be uniform brown. Delicate creature that he is, the kid stands almost from birth but he won't venture far from mother yet. He remains hidden whilst the doe visits him regularly to feed him. Later he follows her and she will play with him. A group can be spotted forming circles and figures-of-eight around one another, rather as the buck will do before mating. The youngster may be steady on its feet but the female never trusts to luck. If she ever has to leave her offspring, she will press its tiny body into a pile of bracken or undergrowth, and camouflage him perfectly until her return.

Horses The horse family, too, readily take to their feet and are born with all senses alert. The brown-striped **zebra** *above* his markings yet to darken, can run about within an hour or two of birth, but remains close to the mother as she grazes in the African grasslands south of the Sahara. His high legs, now folded as he lies, and a very short body already provide the foal with the best possible build for speed. He is, remember, the favourite prey of the lion. Hairy young **donkeys**, like the one shown *right*, also walk early. Rapidly acquired walking skill such as this is linked with the need to stay with the herd as they move about in search of new grazing ground. Usually, the process of standing for the very first time is easily achieved but it is always a fascinating sight. The **pony** *left* will lie with his legs folded inwards, and then lift himself up, hind legs first, to a wobbly upright position. Very soon he will be taking his first unsteady steps.

Goat Sheep and goats are often very hard to distinguish. Both are early developers. The mountain goat kid *above* born in the spring, will be standing upright in under ten minutes and will be jumping around within thirty. Even at this early stage, tiny soft horns are visible and he has an instinctive urge to climb. This is an ability that stands him in good stead in the face of precipitous slopes. In the absence of anything else to scale, he can often be found clambering on to an adult's back!

Opposite
Lambs Sure-footedness has many obvious advantages. The bighorn lamb *top left* lives in mountainous areas with sheer slopes of rock. From an early age he will need nimble footwork to find his way among the rocks and crags, sometimes running with his mother to escape from a wolf or a bird of prey. The other lambs *pictured* also take to their feet when only a few minutes old. Soon they are bounding around, jumping on to their mother as she lies on the ground and playing what seems to be a version of 'king of the castle'. This is educational play and a preparation for adult life.

Left
Gnu Like most infant antelopes, the gnu or wildebeest calf is almost silent. Communication with its mother is therefore restricted to touch—usually via a tug at the udder—and a well-developed sense of smell. Yet in all other ways the calf is independent. Although still being suckled, the pale-skinned youngster will begin to eat grass when one week old.

Below left
Llama Like the baby camel, a new-born Peruvian llama is usually far lighter in colour than the adult but there can be tremendous variation in the shading of their coats. This baby is truly precocious. As soon as the llama is born, it will bound about happily, and quickly adapts itself to its mountainous home in the Andes. A calf will be nursed by its mother for six to twelve weeks. But soon after that the hardy young males will be driven from the herd by the adult females and be forced to join up with a bachelor group. His childhood is brief.

Below
Rhino A young rhinoceros playfully sports with his mother. Even as a new-born baby, the single calf—only twenty inches high and dwarfed by his mother—is very well-developed. Born with a hairy coat and first hidden in a bush, he can stand within the hour. His hearing and sense of smell—for which the adult is renowned—are already very sensitive and, within just a week or two, although still suckling, he has already begun to graze.

Antelopes Many of the antelope family
look like deer, but in fact they form a
classification of their own. They vary
greatly in size. Some are no bigger than
a rabbit: others will be as large as a cow
when they mature. Some live in forests.
Others dwell in the desert or on the
savannah. But, unlike creatures who give
birth to numerous, helpless offspring, the
antelope has only one baby at a time and
this baby is active from birth. The baby
antelope will remain with his mother
while feeding on her milk, but apart from
this nourishment he needs very little care.
He can stand within hours and will run
swiftly with the herd when chased. An
antelope found only in southern Ethiopia,
the **nyala** *right* usually wanders in herds
of up to sixteen, but the doe will be
found alone in the company of her
newborn calf. Here they stand together
at the water's edge, the mother drinking
and the baby looking on, already
well-balanced on his long, slim legs and
with the characteristic white stripes on a
sandy-coloured coat.

Born between November and December
in the scrublands of east and central
Africa, the tiny baby **suni** *top left* is one
of the very smallest antelopes. Even the
fully grown mother is no more than one
foot high at the shoulder. For such a tiny
animal with such a fragile frame, the suni
is admirably active at birth, standing
almost at once and with senses alert to
preying predators like pythons.

The baby **puku** or **waterbuck** *below left*
is a little less steady on his feet, but then
he is only an hour or so old. For the
moment, he stands precariously: but
confidence will soon be developed and
in no time at all he will be very much at
home among the marshy meadows that
form his African habitat.

56

Left
Kongoni The antelope's shiny eyes are not only a striking feature, they are also an indication of his excellent sight. Here, a very young kongoni—one of the smallest of the hartebeestes—sits among the dry African grass, his gleaming eyes protruding from his head. Because of his colouring, he is scarcely noticeable in such an environment. But even at this age he will quickly notice any strange presence, so sharp is his sight and so sensitive his hearing.

Below
Dikdik The baby dikdik is minute. Still and shy, he lies camouflaged in dense vegetation, only his large gleaming eyes providing clues to his whereabouts. So very elusive are these small antelopes, both as infants and in adulthood, that very little is known of their habits and the rearing of their young. From a very early age, however, they are agile. Even new-born, they will bound into the air with amazingly sure-footed leaps when frightened or disturbed.

Opposite
Steinbuck The steinbuck, too, is born well-hidden in grass, with ears and eyes open; and his very shiny nose is clear evidence of the excellent sense of smell that is characteristic of all antelopes. Already he is well equipped with all necessary defensive senses to make him aware of his enemies. But as a departure from general antelope behaviour, the mother steinbuck will keep him hidden in a hole in the ground for a few days after his birth, for extra security when she is grazing for food.

Below
Wild Boars These young wild boar twins are new to the world and yet from the moment of birth they have been able to see and soon to stand on their own four feet. Their pale-brown striped coats contrast clearly with the mother's smooth black hair. These babies are only two weeks old but although they are still suckling, their hunt for food begins. The litter soon learns how to root among the shrubs and bushes.

Opposite top
Wart hogs These wild pigs are far from attractive as adults, but their young make quaint—if strange—babies. Here, lined up at the water's edge, they lower their snouts for a long, cooling drink in the heat of the African sun. Quick to stand and show signs of activity, these piglets nevertheless remain close to their mother. Their father, the boar, is selfish and takes no further notice of them after birth. Often the female can be seen walking along with her offspring in line right behind her, all with tails erect. This is an instinctive signal that the family is on the move and that a single-file procession is the order of the day.

Opposite below
Piglets A litter or 'sounder' of piglets — all pink and patchy—may number up to twenty. All will be sure-footed within the hour. At first they lie semi-crouched, trying hard to rear themselves up with their legs folded inwards and, not unexpectedly, they fail. After several attempts, they eventually stand unsteadily for a moment, only to belly-flop down again. A few minutes later, however, they have mastered that technique and will be tottering about with legs widespread, squeaking noisily and enjoying this early independence. Their squealing is not without purpose: probably it helps to keep the 'sounder' together. The mother, too, will grunt while rooting as a signal to her young and to reassure them.

Cattle The American buffalo calf or bison *below* like all members of the cattle family, takes to the world very quickly. He is born well-developed, and will stand with almost no hesitation. Now he has found his feet, it will be only an hour or so before the endearing brown calf is walking around, close at heel to his darker, powerful mother. The European bison is also born alert but the reddish-brown baby *left* has been caught by the camera before taking to his feet. In only a few seconds, he will rise and prove himself the born-walker that he is, well able to run in the face of danger. The domestic calf *right* is also a precocious youngster. He is born with a full coat and with his eyes wide open, and he is soon able to walk about with confidence. He will suckle from his mother, but otherwise he needs little maternal care.

Unusual babies

Most of the baby animals we have looked at so far have been either hatched or nursed by their mothers. But not all young animals have such a traditional upbringing. The mother cuckoo, for instance, always lays her eggs in the nests of other birds, leaving the enforced foster mothers with full responsibility for rearing her young. Likewise, the baby emu is abandoned by its mother and, as soon as the eggs are laid, it is up to the father bird to hatch and rear his nestlings. Prairie dog pups are also abandoned at a very young age and left to fend for themselves while, in a contrasting behaviour pattern, a baby elephant will be brought up not only by his mother but also by a team of 'aunts'. Read on to find out more about unusual infancies such as these. Baby bears, you will find, are unusual because of their very small size at birth. Read, too, how the hamster, now a very common household pet, was found in fact only as recently as 1930; how the grass rat, by the time it is three months old, may have as many as 30 brothers and sisters; how extremely active the guinea pig is right from birth, although a 'nest baby'; and about the very strange nest into which the baby hare or leveret is born.

Many of the animals in this section are also associated with myths and legends. Everyone knows, of course, the legends connected with the stork — but did you know that elephants have from the very earliest times figured in ancient folklore? The Hindus have a remarkable theory that eight bull and eight cow elephants came from the two halves of a vast egg. They believed that these very first elephants could fly and that they lost the power of flight when one of them was unlucky enough to land on a banyan tree which crashed down and flattened the hut of a holy man or hermit who promptly put a curse on all flying elephants. From that day to this elephants have been unable to fly! In India, too, elephants are regarded as a symbol of grace. Early Indian poets often compare their beloved to an elephant, since the swaying movements of the elephant were supposed to resemble the graceful walk of a beautiful woman.

Although elephants can cause enormous damage when the wild herds break into plantations and trample young trees underfoot, they have proved extremely useful to man, both as beasts of burden and also in a military sense. The ancient Carthaginians used elephants in their wars against the Romans and their vast, armour-clad bodies struck terror into the Roman troops. Perhaps the most famous use of elephants as 'war machines' was by the famous general Hannibal who took his troop of elephants right across the Alps in 218 BC.

It seems a far cry from elephants to hedgehogs, but hedgehogs, too, have their place in myth and legend. The hedgehog's prickly coat is quite a formidable defence system. If a hedgehog is disturbed, it stops in its tracks and raises the spines on its head. If you put your hand near it it may toss its head upwards and hit your hand with the spines, which is uncomfortable. After that, if the hedgehog is still alarmed, it will roll into a ball. One naturalist has claimed that he saw a hedgehog jump as much as a foot into the air. This must be most unusual although baby hedgehogs will often jump a few inches upwards when you touch them. Even their tiny spines can make your skin sting. Hedgehogs can let out quite remarkable screams for their size. When a hedgehog is hurt it screams almost like a baby, but only if caught by the leg.

Country people have long believed that hedgehogs suck milk from cows. Naturalists have long disbelieved this. They say that when a hedgehog has been seen nosing around the udder of a cow lying on the ground it was seeking out insects such as beetles that had crawled under the udder for warmth. They also say that when milk leaks from a cow's teats the hedgehog will come and lick it up, and that this was the reason why farmers and other people thought the hedgehog was actually sucking the milk. A few years ago it was shown beyond doubt that a hedgehog can, and will, suck milk from a cow's teat and in doing so will sometimes bite the teat, injuring it. Apparently it will do this even when a cow is standing up, the hedgehog standing on its hind feet to reach the teat.

Opposite
Storks Throughout the western world the stork is associated with babies and birth although nobody quite knows how the legends began. Certainly the stork has been an omen of good fortune since the earliest times, and many folktales have been woven around him. The Dutch in particular are very superstitious about storks. They say that if a stork builds a nest on your rooftop, he will leave behind one baby when the others fly from the nest. This fledgling, they believe, will bring you luck for life. In Holland, and Germany too, you will notice special platforms built high up on the rooftops of country houses—an open invitation for any passing stork to nest there. Once hatched from their chalky-white eggs, baby storks are first covered with a sparse white down, but this is soon replaced by feathers. Their beaks are black, and the long orange bill does not develop until the bird is mature. Altogether these three fledglings will spend almost two months in the nest and during this time they will be fed by both parents. Storks have a special feeding method. Food is regurgitated on to the nest by the parent and the young then scramble for the bits.

Below

Cuckoo This baby cuckoo is in a nest that is far too small for him and he is being fed by a 'mother' half his size! Really she is his 'foster' mother, for mother cuckoos lay their eggs in the nests of other birds and they leave these other host birds to hatch and rear out their babies. Cuckoos are not the only birds who behave in this curious way. The black-headed duck of South America, for instance, also abandons its eggs, most commonly in the nests of herons and coots. As soon as it is hatched, the young cuckoo calls incessantly, making a shrill sound rather like a very squeaky bicycle pump. Although he in no way resembles them, the foster-parent birds are stimulated by the baby cuckoo's squeaky call, and the sight of his bright red throat,

to feed him whenever he wants. The fledgling cuckoo may be a stranger to the nest, but he certainly won't go hungry. His plaintive call and his brightly coloured throat serve him well. Other passing birds react to them in much the same way, and also stop by to give him food. So from the moment he is hatched, the cuckoo becomes a considerable scrounger. It is part of his nature!

Opposite

Emus These three enchanting baby emus are closely following father's footsteps. Father plays a big role in the life of a baby emu, for once her eggs have been laid, mother emu promptly abandons them. The babies are then incubated, and cared for by the father exclusively. In fact, the male emu is by nature an excellent

mother! He rarely leaves his clutch of 7–10 even to look for food. Ingeniously packed into eggs half as big as their birth size, these cute babies are white when they emerge from their shells, with brown and yellow stripes that eventually mellow. The young will remain with the single parent for as long as a year and a half. Because the emu is flightless, the nest is built on the ground and they are therefore prone to disturbance. As soon as he senses danger, father emu immediately leaves the nest, and as often as not the brood will lead the way. How do they know which path to take? When the brood goes in front of the father, scientists believe that the tone of the adult call provides an accurate signal and directive and, in fact, tells the babies where to go.

Top left

Bears This cuddly black bear cub is sniffing around for food. He seems very independent but until his second summer he will remain close to his mother. He still has a great deal to learn before venturing out alone but many of the skills he requires for facing adult life will be picked up naturally in the course of play. These two young brown bears *below left* may appear to be fighting, but they won't hurt each other since they don't use their claws or teeth and the fighting is always in fun. This sort of rough and tumble is in a way an apprenticeship for adult life in which the cubs are learning to defend themselves. They may also be establishing who will be the natural leaders in later life. The fully-grown brown bear is enormous, weighing-in at up to 1,500 pounds. Her babies—often twins or triplets--are remarkably small, only one two-hundredth the size of their mother. Bear cubs don't leave their den until about three or four months after their birth which usually takes place in January or February. Like most other bears the Syrian cub—*right*, with its mother—is darker than the adult, and is really little better than a podgy ball of flesh. He has the shortest of legs and an almost non-existent neck: so much so that it was once widely believed that mother bears quite literally licked their babies into shape as they lovingly cleaned them! This licking action builds up a strong bond between the mother bear and her babies. And this 'family' feeling also develops the bear's intelligence. Oddly enough bears are closely related to the dog, raccoon and weasel families. There is one very curious thing about bears which some people believe is doubtful, but it is thought that because they love sweet things they are one of the very few wild animals to suffer from bad teeth. Most bears are very quick and agile on their feet, despite their bulk. Some species can reach running speeds of up to thirty miles per hour.

Left

Prairie Dogs The prairie dog is a native of North America's great plains. These two little puppies have just left their burrow for the first time. They stay underground until they are about to be weaned from their mothers. At that stage, they come to the crater-like entrance and face the daylight. Prairie dogs build their burrows close together in extensive colonies or 'towns'. One of these towns, covering an area 100 by 240 miles, was estimated to have a total population of no less than 400,000,000 dogs. Recently, prairie dogs have been largely wiped out. The ground they once burrowed has been tilled and the crater openings destroyed. What really makes these animals unusual, however, is the way in which—like the baby emus—they are abandoned by their mothers. Born April—May, without any fur covering and less than three inches in length, these curious creatures remain blind for at least one whole month. In

late summer, the mother prairie dog moves on and makes a new burrow, leaving her young a ready-made home.

Below left
Elephant The elephant has the longest gestation period of all animals—670 days from conception to birth. But a baby elephant has a splendid mother and even his 'aunts' will help to look after him! Very few people have ever witnessed the birth of a baby elephant in a wild state, and so very little is known about their early days. But it seems that just before the birth, the mother retires to a thicket and is attended there by one or two other females who presumably protect her while the calf is being born. The calf is hairy and by other baby standards is enormous. He weighs, on average, 180–225 pounds in all (that is as much as a full grown man) and he stands three feet high. Yet—see our picture—he is at this stage only around one-third of his adult size. Almost immediately after his

birth he is up on his feet, and within just an hour he can walk around with confidence. As yet, his trunk is short, but this is really just as well, for he uses his mouth to suck from his mother and if his trunk were any longer it would be in the way. Tusks are not yet visible. These come much later on, and will not appear for at least another two years. In colour, right from birth, the elephant takes after his parents.

Below
Hedgehog This baby, like all baby hedgehogs, made an entry into the world from a most unusual angle—he was born on his back! He is a summer baby and is one of a litter numbering anything up to five. But the really intriguing thing about the birth of a baby hedgehog is that his mother is never pricked by him. Before he is born, the baby hedgehog has very tiny pimples on his back, each in a spot where a spine will later grow. These spines do not show through until after

birth, so the mother is not inconvenienced by them. Even when they do first appear they are soft and white, and also they are fewer in number than in the adult. The hedgehog is an independent sort of baby and within minutes after his birth, although he is blind and deaf, he toddles around quite happily on his own and can locate his mother in order to suck since his very keen sense of smell is already well-developed. Father hedgehog has nothing more to do with the female once he has mated with her, so never sees his offspring except by accident. As soon as her litter is born, the female has to search for food and while foraging leaves her babies in a soft nest of grass or leaves. Baby hedgehogs are unable to roll up into a ball until they are eleven days old, since their muscles aren't strong enough until then. There are many legends associated with hedgehogs. One Ancient Greek philosopher believed it was possible to foretell changes in the direction of the wind by watching their movements.

Above

Guinea Pig The colouring of the domesticated guinea pig can vary enormously--plain white, mottled brown, black or burnished orange. But in their native home--in northern South America, where they were first domesticated by the Incas--their soft, smooth fur is usually reddish-brown. Baby guinea pigs are active and well-developed at birth, with bright beady eyes which are already wide open. Within an hour or so they run about quite actively and by the time they are a week old, they will have grown to around one-third their full adult size.

Opposite above

Hare This newly-born brown hare is hardly the size of a man's fist. Although only a few days old he is already independent. His eyes are open at birth, his body is thickly covered with fur and his sense of smell is already acute. His ears are somewhat shorter than the adult's, he has less hair on his underside and his tail is a little less bushy. But in a short time he will resemble his parents. Unlike baby rabbits, hares are born above ground and not in a burrow. Even so the mother never builds an elaborate nest. Instead, she gives birth in a tussock of grass, which is known as a 'form' because the grass becomes pressed to the shape, or form, of the leveret's body. You may sometimes see those strange, flat patches in the grass. These are certain evidence of the recent birth of a litter, but don't be surprised if you don't see the leverets. At first, two or three babies lie together in one form, and here are well-camouflaged, but soon the mother disperses them, each to a form of its own.

Below

Hamsters The hamster--one of the world's most popular domestic pets--has a most surprising history. Incredible as it seems, the millions of golden hamsters kept today have been bred from a single family (a mother and twelve young), dug out of the desert sand in Syria as recently as 1930. The female--shown here with four of a litter which may number many more--gave birth in a nest of dried grass. The young are born helpless, hairless and blind, but they are amazingly vocal very soon after birth. At three days old their backs become black and they start to scurry around the nest, although their eyes are not yet open. By two weeks this small mammal has been weaned. Its eyes are fully open and it is almost fully independent, with a lovely golden coat. From now on, progress is rapid--so rapid that hamster parental responsibilities are very short-lived.

Overleaf

Grass Rat Although he is not yet weaned and is still taking milk from his mother, this silky baby grass rat exercises his jaws by chewing at a grass stem--a first introduction to the adult rat diet. Just because he is alone, don't think that his mother only gives birth to one baby at a time. After the birth of a litter which may number 7–14, the mother rat may immediately mate again and produce a similar brood within the month. Baby grass rats are covered with long, sparse but smooth hair when they are born. The babies are blind at birth but they mature rapidly. Grass rats are to be found in Southern Arabia, and throughout most of Central Africa, where they build underground nests of grass.

Acknowledgements

The publishers would like to thank the following organizations and individuals for their kind permission to reproduce the pictures in this book:

Ardea 43, 54 bottom, 59 top, 70

Bavaria Verlag 41, 68 bottom

Frank Blackburn 7

Camera Press 8 top, 11, 12, 46 bottom, 66 bottom

Bruce Coleman 8 bottom (R Allin), 54 top, 56 bottom (D Bartlett), 31 top right (S Bisserot), 15 top left (R Borland), 15 top right, 17, 18 bottom, 19 bottom, 31 bottom, 47, 49 top, 56 top, 57, 61, 71 bottom, 72 (Jane Burton), 42 bottom (Robert Burton), 32 bottom (R Campbell), 60 bottom (A Deane), 25 (J Dermid), 52 bottom (F Erize), 15 Bottom (P Hinchliffe), 42 top (J Markham), 16 bottom right (E Park), 13 (J. Pearson), 24 (G Pizzey), 9 (G Plage), 2, 26 (M Quarishy), title page (H Reinhard), 50, 51 top left (L Lee Rue), 60 top (J Simon), 68 top (J Van Wormer)

Colour Library International 30, 44, 51 bottom, 55

Jacana 31 top left, 35, 45

Frank Lane 5, 66 top

NHPA 39 (A Anderson), 38 bottom (D Baglin), 36 bottom (A Bannister), 22 bottom (J Clayton), 36 top (S Dalton), 46 top (J Good), 38 top (P Johnson), 28 bottom (I Polunin)

Natural Science Photos 16 bottom left, 33, 53

Okapia 27

PAF 10 bottom